WALKING TOWARD

Eternity

Making Choices For Today

SERIES ONE: DARING TO WALK THE WALK

JEFF & EMILY CAVINS

Journal

ASCENSION
PRESS

West Chester, Pennsylvania

Nihil obstat:	Reverend Robert A. Pesarchick, STD
	Censor Librorum
	February 1, 2012
Imprimatur:	+Most Reverend Charles J. Chaput, O.F.M. Cap.
	Archbishop of Philadelphia
	February 1, 2012

Walking Toward Eternity is a resource of *The Great Adventure* Bible Study Program.

Jeff Cavins, general editor, *The Great Adventure* Bible Study Program; co-author and presenter, *Walking Toward Eternity*
Emily Cavins, co-author, *Walking Toward Eternity*
Sarah Christmyer, editor, *The Great Adventure* Bible Study Program

Ascension Press
Post Office Box 1990
West Chester, PA 19380
Customer service: 1-800-376-0520
AscensionPress.com
BibleStudyforCatholics.com

Printed in Hong Kong

ISBN 978-1-935940-18-0

CONTENTS

From the Authors 1

1. Hearing the Voice of God 3

2. Walking in **Love** 13

3. Walking in **Forgiveness** 29

4. Walking in **Humility** 45

5. Walking in **Prayerfulness** 63

6. Walking in **Faithfulness** 79

7. Walking in **Sacrifice** 95

8. Walking in **Thankfulness** 111

FROM THE AUTHORS

Welcome to *Walking Toward Eternity – Daring to Walk the Walk*. This study grew out of our desire to be more like Christ and to take practical steps to change in key areas. For most of us, lasting change is not easy. Experiencing change, even modest change, is what this study is all about.

This study is different from a typical Bible study. We have designed each lesson to use Scripture as a way to encounter Christ in meditation and prayer. As St. Augustine said, "When we pray, we speak to God; when we read the Scriptures, God speaks to us." We hope that as you study God's Word, your relationship with the Lord will deepen as you continue this intimate conversation with him.

Using the Scriptures and your journal, you will experience daily meditative prayer, which will allow God's Word to work in you to instill the mind of Christ and to obtain the grace necessary for change. Group discussion time will provide community and support, and the lectures will help focus you and challenge you to take action. Because making personal changes can be difficult on our own, these discussion groups will also keep you accountable as you follow through on the commitments you make each week.

The most dynamic aspect of this study is that each week will end with quiet time spent in the Lord's presence, where you will commit to one specific step that you will take. Your journal, group discussions, lectures, and actions will work together to help you grow in the virtues of love, forgiveness, humility, prayer, faithfulness, sacrifice, and thankfulness.

We are glad you can join us as together we dare to "walk the walk."

– Jeff and Emily Cavins

one

HEARING THE VOICE OF GOD

"If you would attain to what you are not yet, you must always be displeased by what you are. For where you are pleased with yourself, there you have remained. Keep adding. Keep walking. Keep advancing."

– St. Augustine

"Yesterday is gone. Tomorrow has not yet come. We only have today. Let us begin."

— *Blessed Teresa of Calcutta (Mother Teresa)*

"If a person meditates consistently on God, a complete revolution takes place in that person's behavior."

— *Archbishop Fulton Sheen*

"In the spiritual life you must take one step forward each day in a vertical line, from the bottom up."

— *St. Pio of Pietrelcina (Padre Pio)*

Session One Outline

DVD Presentation: "Hearing the Voice of God"

This video session will introduce the Walking Toward Eternity *program, explain the various parts of the program, and share what you can expect to get out of it. Add your notes to the talk outline below.*

I. Goal of This Study

    a. Modest change – small steps

    b. Romans 12:2 – "Be transformed," developing the mind of Christ

II. What Makes this Study Different

    a. An encounter with Christ in prayer

    b. Applying God's Word in seven areas of virtue

III. Action is Required for Change

    a. Engaging the will

    b. Hosea 10:12 – "Breaking up unplowed ground"

        i. 2 Kings 4 and 5

        ii. Joel 2

IV. Tools for the Study

    a. Journal

    b. Bookmark

    c. Bible (RSV:CE or NAB) – "One you can live in"

V. The Process

    a. Four days each week

        i. Engage with the topic

  ii. Meditate on the selected Scriptures

  iii. Practice *lectio divina*

  iv. Homework

b. Meeting day

  i.   Learn to pray *lectio divina* as a group

  ii. Share and grow

  iii. Presentation (45–50 min.)

  iv. Point of decision: three questions

    a.) What is God putting his hand on in your life?

    b.) What, specifically, is he asking you to do?

    c.) When will you take the step?

VI. Background of *Lectio Divina*

a. Pope Benedict XVI: *Lectio divina* is "key to new springtime of evangelization" (2008 Synod on Sacred Scripture)

b. St. Augustine and St. Cyprian observed: In prayer, we speak to God; as we read the Bible, we can experience God speaking to us

c. An excellent prayer resource: *Praying Scripture for a Change* by Dr. Tim Gray

VII. *Lectio Divina*: Example, Psalm 23

a. **Read** (*Lectio*)

  i.   Look for details, gather facts, notice key words

  ii. What does the passage say?

b. **Meditate** (*Meditatio*)

  i.   Wonder about what it says

    ii. Engage your mind, don't empty it

        a.) Isaiah 31:4 – a lion "meditates" *(hagah)* over its prey

  c. **Pray** *(Oratio)*

    i. What does this mean to you?

    ii. Respond to God in your words

  d. **Contemplate** *(Contemplatio)*

    i. The result, the fruit – rest in God's presence

  e. Put it into practice *(Operatio)*

VIII. Hearing God's Voice Today

  a. CCC 142, 143 – Submit intellect and will to God; the obedience of faith

  b. Believe that God speaks today

  c. Believe you are capable of hearing him speak to you

  d. Be involved in the Scriptures

  e. Insight from Father Toups

  f. Example: Philip (Acts 8)

IX. Conclusion

  a. Each week, facilitator will ask, "Did you make the change?"

    i. Share as you feel comfortable

    ii. Support one another in prayer

Group Discussion

*During this time you will get acquainted with others in your small group
and learn more about the materials and home study portion of the class.*

Small Group Assignment

Facilitator _____

_____

Phone and/or email _____

_____

Location _____

_____

Walking Together

This study is designed to assist you in moving toward real
change in your life through prayerful daily meditation
on Scripture. The others in your small group are on the
same journey. After you have studied each topic, Jeff
Cavins will encourage you to take one concrete step
to put into practice what you have learned and create
change. Starting next week, the facilitator of your group
will ask a simple question at the beginning of each
discussion time: "Did you take the step?" A simple "yes"
or "no" is all that is needed, but you may share more as
time allows.

We all know how difficult change can be. Please
remember to pray for the others in your group.

How to Use This Journal

1. Home Preparation: Days 1 to 4

This journal will guide you on your daily "walk" as you prepare for the days you meet with your group. The study you do at home is less about learning than it is about hearing from God in his Word, letting that Word come into contact with your life and responding to God in prayer. It is important to spend a small amount of time each day – fifteen to twenty minutes should be sufficient – rather than doing it all at once or at the last minute.

Four days of prayerful reading are outlined for each session. Every day, you will be prompted to think in a different way about the virtue under discussion that week.

Day 1: Meaning

The first day's questions help you discover the meaning of love, forgiveness, humility, or another virtue. Sometimes you will be asked to contrast the dictionary definition or the world's definition with what the Bible says. You may be asked to reflect on how you have experienced this virtue in your life. You will be provided with several Scripture verses to read and think about. Linger over this exercise, allowing the verses to penetrate your mind before recording what stands out to you.

Day 2: Importance

The second day takes this same virtue and turns your focus to why it is important. Are these arbitrary qualities, or does possessing and practicing them make a meaningful difference in life? What might life be like without them? As in Day 1, you will be prompted to read Scripture to learn God's view on the matter. Once again, take time to savor God's Word; don't simply taste it and move on.

Day 3: Practice

The third day is similar to Days 1 and 2, but the questions build on what you have already read and ask you to consider what this virtue looks like in practice. Along with the brief list of verses you are given to read carefully, you will be presented with a longer passage from the Bible that illustrates the virtue in action. You then will be asked to begin thinking of how your own life measures up and to note whether something is standing in the way of change.

Day 4: Praying Scripture for a Change

After three days of thinking about a virtue, Day 4 asks you to enter into a deeper, more personal encounter with the passage that has meant the most to you that week. Using *lectio divina*, you will be asked to prayerfully meditate on your chosen Scripture passage, listening to hear the voice of God speak to you and responding to him in prayer. After the group discussion and DVD presentation, you will once again pray – this time deciding on and committing to the step you will take toward change. (The instructions for *lectio divina* are on the following page.)

Optional Further Reading

Days 1 to 3 each close with a list of additional verses. These are for optional reading, if you have time and want to explore the topic more. Feel free to use a Bible concordance to find even more verses, if you desire.

Notes for Group Discussion

Space has been set aside on each day's page for discussion notes. At the top is a question that summarizes the theme for that day (for example, "What is love?" at the far right of Session 2, Day 1). You need not answer the question at home; it will be used later to guide group discussion of what you have gleaned during the week. The extra space will allow you to add insights you gain that day from other group members.

2. Meeting Day

Each week on your meeting day, a small group discussion and the DVD presentation will help prepare you to take the first step toward walking in a particular virtue. The "Meeting Day" pages of your journal are designed to help with this process.

Small Group Discussion

To help you recall what you have been reading and thinking about that week's topic, you will begin with a brief group exercise of *lectio divina* on a passage that gets to the heart of the topic. Praying with *lectio divina* in a group is a bit different than praying with it in solitude. (Directions for leading a group discussion in *lectio divina* can be found on page 12.)

The majority of the small group time will be spent discussing the insights you have gained. Four general questions are provided that summarize the goals of day. They are repeated on appropriate pages to minimize the need to flip back and forth in your journal during discussion.

Several additional questions are offered to answer if there is time remaining.

DVD Presentation

An outline of the DVD Presentation is included in your journal. Feel free to take additional notes there as desired.

Quiet Time in the Lord's Presence

At the close of the DVD presentation, you will be asked to spend time in quiet prayer – before the Blessed Sacrament if possible – asking the Lord three questions:

– What are you putting your hand on in my life?

– What specifically do you want me to do?

– When?

My Step for the Week

The last journal page for each session contains a "contract" of sorts on which you may record the specifics regarding the step you have determined to take the following week. Write it down and ask God for help as you dare to "walk the walk."

Instructions for *Lectio Divina* ("Divine Reading")

Choose a brief portion of Scripture to meditate on. Spend a few moments in a quiet place preparing your heart and asking God to meet you in his Word. Follow these steps to praying with the Scripture passage you have chosen:

1. **Read** *(Lectio):* Slowly read the verse(s), looking for details. Notice key words; verbs and nouns; anything repeated, compared or contrasted. What does the passage say? Write down words or phrases that stand out to you.

2. **Meditate** *(Meditatio):* Mentally "chew" on key words or images to extract their meaning. Let the words sink in and take hold. What do those words mean? Write down what you discover.

3. **Pray** *(Oratio):* Pay attention to the way your meditation connects with your life and respond to what you find. Talk to God (not "at" him) about this.

4. **Contemplate** *(Contemplatio):* Savor being in God's presence.

5. **Resolve to Act** *(Operatio):* Make a practical resolution by which you hope to walk in the virtue you have been reading about as Christ does.

Leading a Group Exercise of *Lectio Divina*

Choose three people to read the passage out loud and respond as described below.

1. **Open with prayer.**

   Facilitator: Pray in your own words or with these: "Lord, open our minds, our ears, and our hearts, that we may be transformed by your Word." Sit together quietly for a few minutes, quieting your hearts and preparing to hear the living word of God, spoken to you.

2. **Read** *(Lectio):*

   Reader 1: Read the Scripture passage out loud slowly, thoughtfully.

   Group: Listen prayerfully. What did you hear? In the following silence, speak aloud the word or words that stood out to you.

3. **Meditate** *(Meditatio):*

   Reader 2: Read the same passage again, slowly.

   Group: Listen prayerfully while reflecting on how Christ is speaking to you through the text. Allow the Word to speak into your heart, to touch your life. What is he saying to you? Speak it briefly into the silence that follows.

4. **Pray** *(Oratio):*

   Reader 3: Read the passage slowly a final time.

   Group: Listen quietly to God speaking to your hearts; respond silently to him. After a few minutes of silent prayer, you may share with others what is in your heart.

5. **Contemplate** *(Contemplatio):*

   Group: Spend several minutes of quiet rest in God's love.

6. **Close with the Our Father or other prayer.**

two

WALKING IN LOVE

"Our vocation is to belong to Jesus so completely that nothing can separate us from the love of Christ. What you and I must do is nothing less than putting our love for Christ into practice. The important thing is not how much we accomplish, but how much love we put into our deeds every day. That is the measure of our love for God."

– Blessed Teresa of Calcutta (Mother Teresa)

DAY 1   *Date*_____

The Meaning of Love

Pray before you begin. Ask the Lord to show you what love truly is.

1. Look up the word "love" in the dictionary. How is love defined?

    · *a profoundly tender, passionate affection for another*
    · *a feeling of warm personal attachment*

2. Discover what the Bible has to say about love. Read the following
    verses aloud. Read each one again slowly. Repeat it in your mind
    and think about what it says. After each verse, write down the
    words, phrases, or concepts that most stand out to you.

    a. 1 John 3:16 *laid down his life as lay down our lives for our brothers*

    b. 2 John 1:6 *we walk according to his commandments*

    c. 1 Corinthians 13:4-8
        love never fails

3. Circle the word or phrase you wrote down in Question 2 that
    speaks most to you. Why did you choose it?

    love goes on forever

4. Who in your life has been a role model of this kind of love? How and why?

Parents - especially my Dad even after my Mother died I see their love for each other in they way they are looking at each other in a picture I have.

Seeing probably the first time my folks sitting in my dining room crying B/c he didn't know what was wrong with my mother + nothing he could do Knowing he slept on the floor of the living room when we brought my mother home from the hospital because that was as close as he could get to her

"What is love?"

"To love is to will the good of another."

– *Catechism* 1766
(quoting St. Thomas Aquinas)

Optional Further Reading

a. Romans 13:10

b. 1 John 4:18

c. John 15:13

DAY 2   *Date* _____

The Importance of Love

Pray before you begin. Ask the Lord to show you the importance of love.

1. What kind of love does secular society value? List some ways that
    people show love.

    Love of a man + women
    holding hands
    kissing
    caring for each other

    The love of family members

2. Keeping in mind the definition of love you discovered on Day 1,
    how is love important to you? Describe what life without love would
    look like.

    Love is important because without
    the love + support of family + friends
    the difficult times in life would
    be more difficult
    The love of God knowing He is always
    there through prayer
    Love is the listening ear of family
    friends + esp God.

> "God's very being is love. By sending his only Son
> and the Spirit of Love in the fullness of time, God
> has revealed his innermost secret: God himself is an
> eternal exchange of love, Father, Son, and Holy Spirit,
> and he has destined us to share in that exchange."
>
> – *Catechism* 221

3. Discover what the Bible has to say about love's importance. Read the following verses aloud. Read each one again slowly. Repeat it in your mind and think about what it says. After each verse, write down the words, phrases, or concepts that most stand out to you.

   a. Matthew 22:37-39

      love God with your whole heart, soul & mind

   b. Colossians 3:14

      bond of perfection

   c. John 3:16

      God gave us His Son that all who believe will have eternal life

   d. 1 Corinthians 13:2

      If I do not have love I gain nothing

Optional Further Reading

   a. Mark 12:33 *to love Him w/ all your heart, understanding & strength*

   b. 1 John 4:20 *you have to love those you have seen to love God you haven't seen*

   c. 1 John 4:8

      God is love

DAY 3

Date *Sat 5/12*

Walking in Love

Pray before you begin. Ask the Lord to show you what it means to follow him by walking in love.

1. According to the Bible, what does it mean to walk in love? Prayerfully read these verses several times each and meditate on them. Record what stands out to you about love in action.

    a. Romans 12:9-13 *sincere, mutual affection, rejoice in hope persevere in prayer*

    b. Ephesians 5:2 *live in love as Christ loved us*

    c. Matthew 5:43-44 *love your enemies & pray for them*

    d. 1 John 3:18 *show love by deeds & truth*

2. Read the story of the Good Samaritan in Luke 10:25-37. How did the Samaritan walk in love compared to the priest and the Levite? What kinds of things did he do to demonstrate love?

    The Samaritan stopped & cared for the victim where the priest & Levite walked past him.

    • cleaned & bandaged wounds
    • cared for him
    • paid innkeeper to continue to care for him

"What are some practical ways to walk in love?"

3. As you reflect on this story and the verses in question 1, think about how your love for God relates to your relationship with others. Is there something specific you can identify as needing change in your life?

Open up my time to help or visit those in need.

- *love is in our actions*

- *love is sometimes what we don't do*

4. What obstacles or feelings of resistance come up for you when you think about how you are being called to walk in love?

my selfishness for "me time"

Optional Further Reading

a. John 15:16 *"I chose you ..." whatever you ask the Father in my name he may give you*

b. 1 Peter 1:22
   mutual love

c. Ephesians 4:15-16
   grow with Him in every way

d. Romans 8:28
   all things work for good for those who love God

DAY 4   *Date* _____

Praying Scripture for a Change

Pray before you begin. Ask the Lord to show you in what areas he can help you to love as he does.

1. Look back through your journal for the week and select the Scripture that meant the most to you. Look it up in your Bible and decide whether to read it alone or in the context of the surrounding passage. For example, if you select John 15:13, you may want to start with verse 11 or perhaps continue on to verse 17. You can use as little as one word or phrase or as much as a paragraph.

Write the verse and its reference here:

1 Corinthians 13:4-8 Love never fails
vs. 8 10 Love never fails
v. 4-7 Love is patient, love is
kind. It is not jealous, love is
not pompous, it is not inflated.
it is not rude,. it does not
seek its own interests, it is not
quick-tempered, it does not
brood over injury. it does not
rejoice over wrong doings but

2. Using the steps of *lectio divina* on page 11 or on your bookmark, meditate on the Scripture you chose until it turns into prayer and then simply rest in the Lord, trusting that he will help you to take action and make a change in your life.

rejoices with the truth. It bears
Read *(Lectio)*
all things, believes all things,
hopes all things, endures all
things.

Meditate *(Meditatio)*

Continued on next page…

"What did you glean from your *lectio divina*?"

Pray *(Oratio)*

Contemplate *(Contemplatio)*

Resolve to Act *(Operatio)*

MEETING DAY

Taking the First Step

Small Group Discussion

This is the time to share the insights you received this past week and hear from the other members in the group. You will begin with a brief group exercise of lectio divina.

1. Meditate prayerfully as a group on **1 Corinthians 13:1-13.** (Choose three people to look up the passage and read it out loud as described on page 12.) Take no more than ten minutes on this exercise.

2. Answer these questions as a group, sharing insights gleaned from the verses you meditated on this week. (Turn back in your journal to recall what you discovered each day, and use the space provided to add new insights from the group discussion.)

   • What is love? (Day 1)

   • Why is love important? (Day 2)

   • What are some practical ways to walk in love? (Day 3)

   • What did you glean from your *lectio divina?* (Day 4)

3. If there is time, continue the discussion around any of these questions:

   • How did your definition of love and its importance change or expand?

   • Did you observe any real-life examples of someone walking in love?

   • What insights did you gain about how God's love touches your life or about how you show love to others?

Session Two Outline

DVD Presentation: "Walking in Love"

This video session will prepare you to take the first step in walking more consciously in love. Add your notes to the talk outline below.

I. Introduction

   a. Story of Vincent van Gogh and Paul Gauguin
       Van Gogh wanted to capture love in his art

   b. Universal desire to love and be loved perfectly

II. God's Love: *Agape*

   a. The essence of complete self-giving

   b. 1 John 4:8 – God is love *Father loves his Son & the Son loves the Father. Holy Spirit is the very*

   c. CCC 221 – God's in himself is an eternal exchange of love *being of God's inmost secret – God wants us to participate in this love*

   d. Blessed John Paul II: God is not a solitude but a family

   e. *Gaudium et Spes*: Jesus is loved and he loves

   f. John 3:16 – God gave his only Son

III. How *Agape* Is Different

   a. *Agape* chooses the best for another

   b. Goodwill in action

   c. Romans 5:8 – Christ died for us while we were yet sinners

IV. The World Was Made for God's Glory

   a. Psalm 91:1

b. CCC 293 *God did not want to increase his glory, but to show his love*

c. CCC 1 *God is infinitely perfect - he freely created man to share his life + his love for us.*

V. The Cross

a. God's love most clearly seen in the Cross

God so loved his Son

b. Example of love: Sister Teresa

doing what is right

VI. God Loves You Personally

a. You are loved by God just the way you are

b. Because he loves you, he wants to take you to the next step

c. You will never be satisfied without God's love

i. CCC 27 *only in God will you find satisfaction*

ii. St. John of the Cross

iii. Archbishop Fulton Sheen – "Don't search for the ocean of infinite love in the teacup of finite satisfactions."

Once you lose purpose of life you will never find love

VII. Love Is a Theological Virtue

a. Faith, hope, charity

b. Given at baptism

c. Nurtured by the sacraments, prayer, knowledge

d. CCC 1813 – Infused by God's love in our souls

e. Read CCC 1822 – 1826

VIII. You Are Capable of Loving

    a. John 13:35 – Love is the distinguishing mark of a Christian
love one another)

    b. 1 John 4:16-21 – "Perfect love casts out fear" (vs. 18)
we love because He loves us

IX. Loving Like God

    a. Love is a choice *love is a habet - not what we recieve, but what we give*

    b. Love is a habit – "Love is not a perennial, but an annual" (Fr. Benedict Groeschel, C.F.R.) *love is something we have to do repeatedly*

    c. Love is can be commanded

        i. John 13:34 – A new commandment

        ii. Matthew 5:44 – Love your enemies

X. Your Plan for Loving

    a. Accept God's love for you *no matter what - cut your brothers & sisters a break*

    b. Love those who come across your path (Luke 10)
"Good Samaritan" - an opportunity for people to see your love of God

    c. See everyone as a child of God (St. Augustine quote, *Commentary on 1 John*, 7, 9)

XI. Make It a Point to Know God Better

    a. Knowledge leads to love (St. Catherine of Siena quote from *Dialogues*, 85) *the more one loves God the more*

XII. Use 1 Corinthians 13 as a Measure in Your Life

Quiet Time in the Lord's Presence

This is an opportunity for you to sit and pray silently in Christ's presence, allowing him to speak to your heart about how you can walk in love in new ways. Respond by committing to a specific step you will take to bring about a needed change in your life. **Follow the guidelines on the next page.**

Remember, mental acknowledgement that change is needed is not change. Action – responding in word and deed – is essential for lasting change.

> *"Be renewed in the spirit of your minds, and put on the new man, created after the likeness of God in true righteousness and holiness."*
>
> *– Ephesians 4:23-24*

Walking Together

Remember to pray for the other members of your group during the coming week, knowing that they will be praying for you, too.

My Step for This Week...

1. I believe the Lord is asking me to walk in love toward this
    person (or in this situation) in my life:

    *To walk toward understanding
    why this co-worker acts as if
    I don't exist or know what I
    am doing*

2. Specifically, I am going to do the following in the coming week:

3. I will take the necessary first step on

    _____.
    (day and time)

4. My prayer for help:

    *Oh God please help me to
    be more understanding
    in my thoughts & feelings
    toward this person.*

three

WALKING IN FORGIVENESS

"To be a Christian means to forgive the inexcusable, because God has forgiven the inexcusable in you."

– C.S. Lewis

DAY 1   Date _____

The Meaning of Forgiveness

Pray before you begin. Ask the Lord to show you what forgiveness truly means.

1. Why and when would most people say forgiveness is necessary? Is there ever a time when it is OK not to forgive?

    If they hurt someone by word or action. I feel a lot of times "I'm sorry" is said out of reflect with no meaning or being fully sorry for what they said or did

2. Discover what the Bible has to say about forgiveness. Read the following verses aloud. Read each one again slowly. Repeat it in your mind and think about what it says. After each verse, write down the words, phrases, or concepts about forgiveness that most stand out to you.

    a. Jeremiah 31:34 *'all shall know me I will forgive their evil doing • not remember their sins*

    b. Matthew 26:28 *my blood shed for many forgiveness of sin*

    c. Luke 17:4 *forgive 77x's for 7 wrongs forgive him*

    d. Matthew 6:12, 14-15 *If you forgive others your heavenly Father will forgive you If you don't forgive, Heavenly Father will not forgive you*

3. Circle the word or phrase you wrote down in Question 2 that speaks most to you. Why did you choose it?

    Matthew 6:12, 14-16 forgive other

    Forgiveness is not complete unless you forgive those who hurt you or hurt those you love. + You cannot go on & put the incident behind you until you forgive them + thus go on with your life.

"What does it mean
to truly forgive?"

4. Reflect upon an instance where someone
forgave you or you forgave someone for an
offense. What impact did that have on you
and your relationship with that person?

*Once I verbalized & forgave
the person not directly
to that person, but in confession
I was able to move on to
new career choices & I was
finally able to go to social
events I had previously
avoided if I knew he would
be there.*

*Recently - I have had to
confront anger with other
people that I have to
resolve.*

> "In refusing to forgive our brothers and
> sisters, our hearts are closed and their
> hardness makes them impervious to the
> Father's merciful love; but in confessing our
> sins, our hearts are opened to his grace."
>
> – *Catechism* 2839-2840

Optional Further Reading

a. Hebrews 9:22 *purified by blood
'w/out shedding of blood there
would be no forgiveness)*

b. Hebrews 8:12
*forgive evil doing
remember - sin no more*

c. Colossians 3:12-13
*'heartfelt compassion
· patience
; as the Lord has forgiven you - so must
you forgive others*

DAY 2

The Importance of Forgiving Others

Pray before you begin. Ask the Lord to show you the importance of forgiving others.

1. Describe some patterns or attitudes that result when a person chooses not to forgive.

    - people pull away from each other
    - blame each other
    - severe ties (not communicate
    - act as if the other person doesn't exist

2. Discover what the Bible has to say about the importance forgiving others. First, read the following verses aloud. Then read each one again slowly. Repeat it in your mind and think about what it says. After each verse, write down the words, phrases, or concepts that most stand out to you.

    a. Mark 11:25 to be forgiven by God you need to forgive those who you have a grievance about

    b. Proverbs 19:11
        slow to anger
        overlook an offense

    c. Romans 12:19
        do not look for revenge
        "Vengeance is mine." says the Lord

    d. Matthew 18:21-35
        - forgive 77 x's - unlimited times
        - be patient with me.
        - moved w/ compassion

(margin note, rotated:) d. if you don't forgive your brother our Heavenly Father will withdraw His forgiveness at the final judgment

3. If someone wrongs me and doesn't apologize, why should I forgive that person?

Forgiveness should is a 2 way. street. If not you should still forgive the person who wronged you - so our Heavenly Father will forgive you. It may be necessary to repeat the forgiveness if you still have or the thoughts of the wrong keep resurfacing.

"It is not in our power not to feel or to forget an offense; but the heart that offers itself to the Holy Spirit turns injury into compassion and purifies the memory in transforming the hurt into intercession."

– *Catechism* 2843

Optional Further Reading

a. Ephesians 4:32 *be kind compassionate + forgiving as God has forgiven us.*

b. Luke 6:37 *If you don't judge you wont be judged If you don't condemn you wont be condemned forgive + you will be forgiven*

c. Romans 12:20-21 *Conquer evil with good.*

DAY 3

*Date*_____

Walking in Forgiveness

Pray before you begin. Ask the Lord to show you what it means to follow him by walking in forgiveness.

1. According to the Bible, what does it mean to walk in forgiveness? Prayerfully read these verses several times each and meditate on them. Record what stands out to you about how we are to forgive others:

   a. Matthew 5:44

   love your enemies pray for them

   b. Proverbs 20:22

   Trust in the Lord

   c. 2 Timothy 4:16

   no one appeared on my behalf deserted me dont hold it against them

   d. Matthew 5:23-24

   reconcile with your brother - then offer your gifts at the altar

2. Read Joseph's story in Genesis 50:15-21. What did Joseph do to show that he forgave his brothers, and what does this say to you about God's forgiveness? What effect did this have on both Joseph and his brothers?

   Joseph provided for his brothers & children. He told them that even though they meant to harm him - God had meant it to end in good

   Joseph & his brothers lived together

"*Attachment to a hurt arising from a past event blocks the inflow of hope into our lives.*"

– *St. John of the Cross*

> "How can you forgive someone else, especially when they are not sorry for hurting you?"

3. As you reflect on this story and the verses in Question 1, think about your experience of receiving forgiveness and extending it to others. How has your life been impacted by forgiveness or a lack of forgiveness?

Mentally + in Reconciliation Forgiving the person's who wronged me allowed me to proceed into new areas of my life.

4. When you think about where you are being called to walk in forgiveness, what obstacles or feelings of resistance do you experience?

① The obstacle, the fear/ anxiety of going to this person, that I should personaley speak to the person who did not stand up in defense of me

② The fear that speaking to this person may sever the fragile ties of my son w/ his fathers family. The neglect + lack of feeling James Uncle had for his nephew on the

Optional Further Reading *loss of his father + not guiding him.*

a. Acts 7:59-60
Lord Jesus recieve my spirit. Lord do not hold this sin against them — Stephen

b. Luke 15:11-32
Like our Heavenly Father the father will forgive us if we ask for forgiveness + are truly sorry

DAY 4   *Date* _____

Praying Scripture for a Change

Pray before you begin. Ask the Lord to show you what areas he can help you to forgive as he does.

1. Look back through your journal for the week and select the Scripture that meant the most to you. Look it up in your Bible and decide whether to read it alone or in the context of the surrounding passage.

Write the verse(s) and reference here:

Ephesians 4:32
And be kind to one another,
compassionate, forgiving one
another as God has forgiven
you in Christ.

2. Using the steps of *lectio divina*, meditate on the Scripture you chose until it turns into prayer and then simply rest in the Lord, trusting that he will help you to take action and make a change in your life.

Read *(Lectio)*

Meditate *(Meditatio)*

"What did you
glean from your
lectio divina?"

Continued on next page…

Pray *(Oratio)*

Contemplate *(Contemplatio)*

Resolve to Act *(Operatio)*

MEETING DAY

*Date*_____

Taking the First Step

Small Group Discussion

This is the time to share the insights you received this past week and hear from the other members in the group. You will begin with a group exercise of lectio divina.

1. Meditate prayerfully as a group on **Matthew 18:21-35**. (Choose three people to look up the passage and read it out loud as described on page 12.)

2. Answer these questions as a group, sharing insights gleaned from the verses you meditated on this week. (Turn back in your journal to recall what you discovered each day, and use the space provided to add new insights from the group discussion.)

    *   What does it mean to truly forgive? (Day 1)

    *   Why is forgiving others so important? (Day 2)

    *   How can you forgive someone else, especially when they are not sorry for hurting you? (Day 3)

    *   What did you glean from your *lectio divina*? (Day 4)

3. If there is time, continue the discussion around any of these questions:

    *   How did your definition of forgiveness and its importance change or expand?

    *   Did you observe any real-life examples of forgiveness in action?

    *   What insights did you gain about God's forgiveness in your own life or about how you forgive others?

Session Three Outline

DVD Presentation: "Walking in Forgiveness"

This video session will prepare you to take the first step in walking more consciously in forgiveness. Add your notes to the talk outline below.

I. Introduction

    a.   John 16:33 – We always will have problems, but Jesus has overcome the world

    b.   Stumbling block: *Skandalon* in Greek

        i.   That which gives offense; object of anger or disappointment

        ii.   Traps – Bait goes on the *skandalon*

II. What Happens When We Do Not Forgive

    a.   Israel's pattern

    b.   Exodus 7:16 – "Let my people go!"

    c.   Jeremiah 34:11-21 – Failure to release leads to exile

III. Christ Forgives Us

a. Luke 4:18-19 – Christ proclaims the Great Jubilee

b. Christ paid the price

    i. 1 Peter 1:18-19 – Ransomed by his precious blood

    ii. Matthew 27:21 – Barabbas and Jesus

    iii. John 19:30 – "It is finished."

IV. We Are Called to Forgive as Christ Forgave

a. Matthew 6:12 – Forgive us as we forgive others

b. Example of forgiveness as a choice: Janet

V. Parable of the Unmerciful Servant: Matthew 18:21-35

a. Vs. 21 – Forgive 70 x 7 times

b. Unforgiveness: "It is not finished."

    c. Manifestations of unforgiveness

    d. Example of forgiveness as a daily dying to self: Lynn

    e. Forgiveness resides in the will

    f. Failure to forgive keeps us and others in bondage

VI. Conclusion

    a. 1 Peter 5:7 – "Cast all your anxieties on him, for he cares about you."

    b. We extend the love of God by forgiving others

Quiet Time in the Lord's Presence

*This is an opportunity for you to sit and pray silently in Christ's presence, allowing him to speak to your heart about how you can experience and extend forgiveness in new ways. Respond by committing to a specific step you will take to bring about a needed change in your life. **Follow the guidelines on the next page.***

Remember, mental acknowledgement that change is needed is not change. Action – responding in word and deed – is essential for lasting change.

> *"Be renewed in the spirit of your minds, and put on the new man, created after the likeness of God in true righteousness and holiness."*
> *– Ephesians 4:23-24*

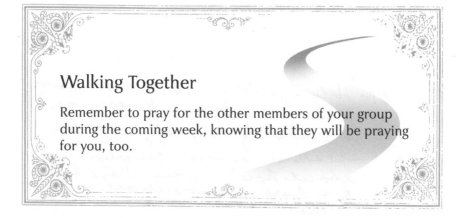

Walking Together

Remember to pray for the other members of your group during the coming week, knowing that they will be praying for you, too.

My Step for This Week...

1. I believe the Lord is asking me to walk in forgiveness toward this person in my life:

   Stephen

2. Specifically, I am going to do the following this week:

   Tell him how I feel about how he has neglected James. Out of ignorance or not caring having the whole estate situation come to the head that is happening now.

3. I will take the necessary first step on

   _____.

   (day and time)

4. My prayer for help:

   Oh Holy Spirit guide me in using the correct words. Guide me in controling my anger a speak to Stephen calmly about how I feel. how he has hurt James + ultimately me.

four

WALKING IN HUMILITY

"If you are humble nothing will touch you, neither praise nor disgrace, because you know what you are."

– Blessed Teresa of Calcutta (Mother Teresa)

DAY 1   *Date* _____

The Meaning of Humility

Pray before you begin. Ask the Lord to show you what humility truly means.

1. What comes to mind when you think of humility? List any positive
    or negative associations.

    - Someone who is not proud
    - to be grounded

2. How would you define the difference between true humility and
    false humility?

    false humility → underrating one
    own value

3. Discover what the Bible has to say about humility. Read the
    following verses aloud. Read each one again slowly. Repeat it in
    your mind and think about what it says. After each verse, write
    down the words, phrases, or concepts about humility that most
    stand out to you.

    - lowly tremble at my word

    a. Isaiah 66:2
    - my hand made all these says the Lord
    - I approve

    b. Matthew 11:29 learn from me
    - I am meek + humble
    - find rest

    c. Philippians 2:5-8 form of God - not equal to God
    - taking form of a slave - came in human
    - likeness, humble himself - obedient - death on a cross

    d. Romans 12:3
    - do not think oneself more highly than one
      ought to think
    - think soberly
    - faith that God has apportioned to you

4. Circle the word or phrase you wrote down
   in Question 3 that speaks most to you.
   Why did you choose it?

   That you shouldn't rate self as "better" than others — act the way God has planned for you.

   - *Humility is being grounded in yourself*
   - *Humility is recognizing your weakness*

5. Jesus said, "I am gentle and lowly in heart."
   List some of the ways that Jesus manifested
   humility during his time on earth.

   Marriage feast of Cana — my time is not now

Optional Further Reading

   a. James 4:6 *grace to the humble
      He bestows grace*

   b. Proverbs 11:2
      *prideful will have disgrace
      humble will have pride*

   c. Proverbs 16:18-19
      - *better to be humble*
      - *pride can lead you to disaster*

DAY 2   *Date* _____

The Importance of Being Humble

Pray before you begin. Ask the Lord to show you the importance of humility.

1. Describe some consequences that can result when a person exhibits pride instead of humility. Give a specific example.

One who acts as if he/she knows "everything" + won't listen when someone tries to explain how they think something should be done or explains how the idea or plan is wrong - In the end the idea or plan is incorrect + has to be redone-rethought or corrected. Causing double work or problems that could have been avoided.

2. Discover what the Bible has to say about the importance of humility. Meditate on the following verses. First, read each verse aloud. Then read it again slowly. Repeat it in your mind and think about what it says. After each verse, write down the words, phrases, or concepts that most stand out to you.

   a. Luke 16:15 justify yourself
      God knows your heart
      human esteem - abomination in eyes of God
   b. Micah 6:8 walk humbly w/your God
      love goodness
   c. James 4:10 humble yourself
      he will exalt you

3. Circle the word or phrase you wrote down in Question 2 that speaks most to you. Why did you choose it?

You can justify what you do or don't do for whatever reason, but God knows the real reason you acted the way you did

4. Many people in our society embrace self-sufficiency and pride as positive strengths, and they see humility as a weakness. How would you answer someone who feels this way?

Those who feel self-sufficiency & pride are positive strengths I would tell them that needing help is not a sign of weakness but rather a strength of humility knowing when you need help

---

"To become a child in relation to God is the condition for entering the kingdom. For this, we must humble ourselves and become little."

– *Catechism* 526

Optional Further Reading

a. Mark 9:35 *"first will be last + servant of all" –. don't think you are better than everyone, but help others*

b. Ezekiel 28:17

c. Matthew 5:5 *meek inherit the earth (Lord) footnote: land refers to the kingdom.*

DAY 3   *Date* _____

Walking in Humility

Pray before you begin. Ask the Lord to show you what it means to follow him by walking in humility.

1. According to the Bible, what does it mean to walk in humility? Prayerfully read these verses several times each and meditate on them. Record what stands out to you about how we are to be humble:

   a. Romans 12:6 *use & share the gifts given me*

   b. 1 Peter 5:5 *God opposes the proud / God bestows favor on the humble / subject yourself to the presbters*

   c. Philippians 2:3 *regard others as more important than yourself*

   d. Luke 14:8-11 *exalt yourself & you will be humble / humble yourself & be exalted*

2. Read the story of the Pharisee and the Tax Collector in Luke 18:9-14. What does this parable say about walking in pride versus walking in humility? *" be merciful to me a sinner" That you should humble yourself to God about your sinfulness & dependence on God for forgiveness because if you feel you are above sin then you are not being honest with yourself.*

"*Pride makes us artificial. Humility makes us real.*"

– *Thomas Merton*

"What are some
practical ways to
walk in humility,
especially when you
don't feel like it?"

3. As you reflect on this story and the verses in Question 1, is there a situation in your life where a lack of humility is causing problems? Is there something specific you can identify as needing change in your life?

Sometimes in the work situation I am better than some co-workers because I continue to work while the visit + complain about our boss (which I try to stay away from. All these are inner thoughts + I need to think about times when I have "milked the clock"

4. What obstacles or feelings of resistance come up for you when you think about how you are being called to walk in humility?

An obstacle to be overcome is spending more time in charitable or volunteer activities than think "my" time is more important. In todays society people put an importance on showing how good they are, that they can do something better than others. So an obstacle would be to try + not "toot my own horn" + and ask for help

Optional Further Reading

a. Ephesians 4:2 *v.1 worthy of your call v.2 w/ humility, gentleness, + patience through love*

b. Matthew 21:5 *King shows his humility riding on an ass (beast of burden)*

c. 1 Peter 2:23 *do not return insults did not threaten when He suffered*

DAY 4

Praying Scripture for a Change

Pray before you begin. Ask the Lord to show you in what areas he can help you to be humble, as he is.

1. Look back through your journal for the week and select the Scripture that meant the most to you. Look it up in your Bible and decide whether to read it alone or in the context of the surrounding passage.

Write the verse and its reference here: Ephesians 4:2 (1-4)
I ... urge you to live in a manner worthy of the call you have received with all humility and gentleness, with patience, bearing with one another through love, striving to preserve the unity of the spirit through the bond of peace

2. Using the steps of *lectio divina*, meditate on the Scripture you chose until it turns into prayer and then simply rest in the Lord, trusting that he will help you to take action and make a change in your life.

Read *(Lectio)*

Meditate *(Meditatio)*

"What did you
glean from your
lectio divina?"

Continued on next page…

Pray *(Oratio)*

Contemplate *(Contemplatio)*

Resolve to Act *(Operatio)*

MEETING DAY

Date _____

Taking The First Step

Small Group Discussion

This is the time to share the insights you received this past week and hear from the other members in the group. You will begin with a group exercise of lectio divina.

1. Meditate prayerfully as a group on **Philippians 2:5-8.** (Choose three people to look up the passage and read it out loud as described on page 12.)

2. Answer these questions as a group, sharing insights gleaned from the verses you meditated on this week. (Turn back in your journal to recall what you discovered each day, and use the space provided to add new insights from the group discussion.)

   • What does it mean to be humble? (Day 1)

   • Why is humility important? (Day 2)

   • What are some practical ways to walk in humility, especially when you don't feel like it? (Day 3)

   • What did you glean from your *lectio divina*? (Day 4)

3. If there is time, continue the discussion around any of these questions:

   • Did you observe any real-life examples of humility in action?

   • What do you see as the benefits of being humble? List some results of a lack of humility that you might not have recognized before.

   • If you have children, what are some ways you can set an example of humility for them?

Session Four Outline

DVD Presentation: "Walking in Humility"

This video session will prepare you to take the first step in walking more consciously in humility. Add your notes to the talk outline below.

VII. Introduction

    a. Humility frees you to be who you really are *know thyself - be aware of your limitations*

        i. Quote from Juan Luis Lorda, *The Virtues of Holiness* *nothing separates one more from God than lack of humility*

    b. The first step: knowledge of oneself (St. John of the Cross, *The Spiritual Canticle*, 4,1) *to reach a full knowledge of God one needs to know oneself*

VIII. Definition of Humility

    a. Meek, teachable, modest

    b. "Of the earth, grounded"

    c. "Keeping oneself within one's own balance" (St. Thomas Aquinas) *reach out to someone superior to yourself. humility is recognizing your weakness*

    d. Thinking with sober judgment (Romans 12:3)

    e. Responding with humility: Herb Brooks, Connie

    f. Training is required (CCC 2540) *a baptized person needs to train oneself in humility*

    g. Archbishop Fulton Sheen – Positive and negative sides of humility *- keep one from overlooking your mark +*

IX. Humility's Opponent Is Pride

    a. Living as though God does not exist ("Practical atheism," Blessed John Paul II) *Genesis 2:17 sin has a basis in pride*

b. Disordered self-trust (St. Thomas Aquinas)

c. Lucifer's prideful fall (Ezekiel 28:17; Isaiah 14:13-14)

lack of humility changed Lucifer into Satan

d. The Fall led to self-centeredness

X. Jesus: Our Example of Humility

a. Humility is seeing through the eyes of Christ

sin is a grasping at what is not us

   i. Matthew 11:29 *"take yoke upon me"* *yoke of obedience*

   ii. Philippians 2:8

humbled himself - obedient even to death on a cross

b. Every aspect of Christ's life showed humility

   i. The Incarnation - *God sending his Son as a human*

   ii. CCC 564 – "The silent years" - *growing up obedient to Mary & Joseph*

   iii. Matthew 3:13-15 – Baptism *by John at the Jordon River - lowest point on earth*

   iv. CCC 566 – Temptation in the wilderness *resisted temptation of the devil*

   v. Matthew 18:4 – Importance of childlikeness *to be humble like a child is the greatest in the kingdom*

   vi. John 13:1-17 – Washing disciples' feet

XI. Humility Is a Fruit of the Holy Spirit

a. James 4:10 *fruit of the Holy Spirit - humility*

b. Luke 1:46-49 – The Magnificat *humility of Mary*

XII. Scriptures Teach Us about Humility

a.   Key to gaining wisdom – Proverbs 11:2 *When we humble ourself to God we gain wisdom*

b.   God works through the humble – Isaiah 66:2

c.   Ability to diffuse arguments – Proverbs 15:1 *soft answers turn away wrath*

d.   No hypocrisy – Luke 12:1 *Greek – hypocrite means actor*

XIII. Suggestions for Walking In Humility

• sacrament puts everything in perspective

a.   Routine confession – Luke 18:9-14 *• self honestly*
• talking directly to Christ
• daily exam of conscience

b.   Don't exalt yourself – Luke 14:10

c.   Seek the good of others *set aside competition w/ people*
• envy goes against humility

d.   Don't look at outer appearances

e.   Choose to serve others

f.   Be quick to forgive *forgiveness is the greatest step in humility*

g.   Treat pride by embracing the Cross – Luke 9:23 *focus on the demands of daily Christian existence*

  i.   Example of humility; Kitty and Carl *2 Corinthians 12: 1-10*

h.   Pray the Litany of Humility (see page 61)

XIV. Conclusion

Walking in humility is following in God.

Quiet Time in the Lord's Presence

This is an opportunity for you to sit and pray silently in Christ's presence, allowing him to speak to your heart about how you can grow in humility. Respond by committing to a specific step you will take to bring about a needed change in your life. **Follow the guidelines on the next page.**

Remember, mental acknowledgement that change is needed is not change. Action – responding in word and deed – is essential for lasting change.

"Be renewed in the spirit of your minds, and put on the new man, created after the likeness of God in true righteousness and holiness"

– Ephesians 4:23-24

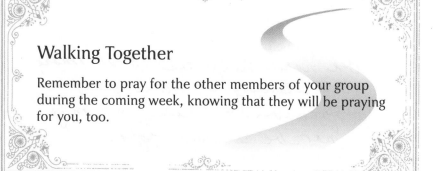

Walking Together

Remember to pray for the other members of your group during the coming week, knowing that they will be praying for you, too.

My Step for This Week...

1. I believe the Lord is asking me to walk in humility in this area of my life:

   Thinking & sometimes ~~ther~~ saying " you're wrong & I am right. That is not what is going on.

2. Specifically, I am going to do the following this week:

   Be patient & not criticize those + ideas I think are wrong because they are different than mine.

3. I will take the necessary first step on

   _____.

   (day and time)

4. My prayer for help:

   Oh Lord help me to be more understanding of other people's opinions & realize I may not be always right.

Litany of Humility

O Jesus! meek and humble of heart, hear me.

From the desire of being esteemed,
Deliver me, Jesus.

From the desire of being loved...
From the desire of being extolled...
From the desire of being honored...
From the desire of being praised...
From the desire of being preferred to others...
From the desire of being consulted...
From the desire of being approved...
From the fear of being humiliated...
From the fear of being despised...
From the fear of suffering rebukes...
From the fear of being calumniated...
From the fear of being forgotten...
From the fear of being ridiculed...
From the fear of being wronged...
From the fear of being suspected...

That others may be loved more than I,
Jesus, grant me the grace to desire it.

That others may be esteemed more than I...
That, in the opinion of the world, others
may increase and I may decrease...
That others may be chosen and I set aside...
That others may be praised and I unnoticed...
That others may be preferred to me in everything...
That others may become holier than I,
provided that I may become as holy as I should...

– Rafael Cardinal Merry del Val (1865-1930),
Secretary of State for Pope St. Pius X

five

WALKING IN PRAYERFULNESS

"For me, prayer is an upward leap of the heart, an untroubled glance toward heaven, a cry of gratitude and love which I utter from the depths of sorrow as well as from the heights of joy."

— *St. Thérèse of Lisieux*

DAY 1
Date _____

The Meaning of Prayer

Pray before you begin. Ask the Lord to show you what prayer truly means.

1. If someone asked you to define prayer, how would you answer that person?

   Prayer is not just talking to God, rather it is having a conversation with God and LISTENING to what he is saying

2. Discover what the Bible has to say about prayer. Read the following verses aloud. Read each one again slowly. Repeat it in your mind and think about what it says. After each one, write down the words, phrases, or concepts about prayer that most stand out to you.

   a. Psalm 62:8 *safety with God*
      my rock
      my refuge

   b. James 4:8 *draw near to God & he will draw near to you*

   c. Matthew 7:7-8 *ask → receive*
      seek → find
      knock → door open to you
      God will open the door to Heavenly life

   d. Hebrews 13:15 *continually offer God praise*
      confess his name

3. Circle the word or phrase you wrote down in Question 2 that speaks most to you. Why did you choose it?

   James 4:8
   The closer you try to get of God through prayer the easier it will be to talk with Him + He will draw you closer.
   Praying with pure thoughts will open your heart and let God in.

"What does it mean to
be a person of prayer?"

4. Who in your life has taken the time to pray
   with you? What was it about their example
   that you found appealing or meaningful?

"Prayer is the raising of one's mind
and heart to God or the requesting
of good things from God."

– *Catechism* 2559

Optional Further Reading

a. Psalm 46:10 — *pray to stop ware, break bows, splinter shields speare, burn shield* ✓ *refers to works of the Lord*

b. Psalm 143:8 — *hear your kindness - show me the path - you I trust - you I entrust my life*

c. Matthew 18:19-20 — *two agree for which to pray - will be granted by Heavenly Father*

DAY 2   *Date* _____

The Importance of Prayer

Pray before you begin. Ask the Lord to show you the importance of prayer.

1. How often and where do you pray? What kind of connection does it
    have to your daily life?

    *Daily - Morning Offering + Prayer to Guardian
    Angel upon waking up*

    Magnificat Prayers in Morning + Evening

    *Rosary - daily either in morning afta
    Mass or evening Before
    going to bed*

    *Act of Contrition - in bed Before going
    to sleep*

    *I feel it "book ends" my day talking
    w/ God. In the last 6-9 months I have
    tried to make prayer a daily part of my
    life where Before it was as a need bas*

2. Discover what the Bible has to say about the importance of prayer,
    meditate on the following verses. First, read the following verses
    aloud. Then read each one again slowly. Repeat it in your mind and
    think about what it says. After each verse, write down the words,
    phrases, or concepts that most stand out to you.

    ✗ a. Mark 11:24 *believe - all you ask in
          prayer
          you will receive + it shall be yours*

    b. Matthew 6:6 *pray in secret
        Father will repay you in secret*

    c. James 4:2 *covet but do not possess
        do not possess Because you did not ask
        ("failure to pray properly"*

    d. 1 Timothy 2:1-2
        • *prayer to be offered for all in authority*
        • *leads to a quiet + tranquil life in
          all*
        • *devotion + dignity*

3. How do you respond when it seems that one of your prayers is not answered?

"Jesus thirsts; his asking arises from
the depths of God's desire for us.
Whether we realize it or not, prayer is
the encounter of God's thirst with ours.
God thirsts that we may thirst for him."

– Catechism 2560

Optional Further Reading

a. Psalm 63:5-6, 8 *bless you as long as I live call on your name, lips honor you, you are my life, I shout for joy*

b. Hebrews 4:16 *confidently approach the throne receive mercy, find grace for help*

c. James 5:16 *confess sins to one another pray for one another – healed fervent prayer is powerful*

d. John 4:14 *water given ... welling up to eternal life.*

DAY 3

Walking in Prayer

Pray before you begin. Ask the Lord to show you what it means to follow him by walking in prayer.

1. According to the Bible, what does it mean to walk in prayer? Prayerfully read these verses several times each and meditate on them. Record what stands out to you about how we are to pray.

   a. Philippians 4:6 *no anxiety thanksgiving make requests to God*

   b. 1 Thessalonians 5:16-18 *rejoice give thanks pray without ceasing*

   c. Mark 1:35 *rise early go to deserted place & pray*

   d. Romans 8:26 *Spirit comes to the aid of our weakness Spirit intercedes we do not know how to pray*

2. Read Jonah's prayer in Jonah 2:1-10. Which elements in this prayer can you identify with? What can you learn from Jonah's experience?

   v. 3 out of my distress I called to the Lord & he answered me

   • I cried for help & you heard my voice

   • That no matter what happens to you God the Father will be with you

---

"We cannot achieve our human fulfillment without communing with God – and the deeper our prayer, the deeper our fulfillment."

– Fr. Thomas Dubay, S.M.

3. As you reflect on this story and the verses in Question 1, can you think of an area in your life where you have been seeking answers from a source other than God? Are there situations where you became overwhelmed and tried to solve the problem as though God did not exist?

"What are practical ways to pray, especially when you don't feel like it?"

4. What obstacles or feelings of resistance come up for you when you think about establishing a life of prayer? *Not necessarily an obstacle, but a different feeling in my spiritual life. In the past it has been a more "hit or miss" type of praying. When I had time, thought of doing it, or when asking for something. Now I am trying to set aside a time or routine for praying*

Optional Further Reading

a. Proverbs 15:9 *he loves the man who pursues virtue.*

b. Isaiah 58:9 *call ... the Lord will answer. Cry for help -.. he will say "Here I am"*

c. 1 John 5:14-15 *confidence - if we ask, he hears us. what we have asked him for is ours*

d. Ephesians 6:18 *pray - every opportunity in the Spirit*

DAY 4   *Date* _____

Praying Scripture for a Change

Pray before you begin. Ask the Lord to show you what areas of your prayer life need to become more like that of Jesus.

1. Look back through your journal for the week and select the Scripture that meant the most to you. Look it up in your Bible and decide whether to read it alone or in the context of the surrounding passage.

Write the verse and its reference here:

Romans 8:26
In the same way, the Spirit too comes
to the aid of our weakness, for we
do not know how to pray as we
ought, but the Spirit intercedes
with inexpressible groanings.
27 And the one who searches hearts, knows
what is the intention of the Spirit, because
it intercedes for the holy ones according
to God's will.

2. Using the steps of *lectio divina*, meditate on the Scripture you chose until it turns into prayer and then simply rest in the Lord, trusting that he will help you to take action and make a change in your life.

Read *(Lectio)*

Meditate *(Meditatio)*

"What did you glean from your *lectio divina*?"

Continued on next page…

Pray *(Oratio)*

Contemplate *(Contemplatio)*

—

Resolve to Act *(Operatio)*

Meeting Day *Date* _____

Taking the First Step

Small Group Discussion

This is the time to share the insights you received this past week and hear from the other members in the group. You will begin with a group exercise of lectio divina.

1. Meditate prayerfully as a group on **Matthew 7:7-8.** (Choose three people to look up the passage and read it out loud as described on page 12.)

2. Answer these questions as a group, sharing insights gleaned from the verses you meditated on this week. (Turn back in your journal to recall what you discovered each day, and use the space provided to add new insights from the group discussion.)

    *   What does it mean to be a person of prayer? (Day 1)

    *   Why is prayer important? (Day 2)

    *   What are some practical ways to pray, especially when you don't feel like it? (Day 3)

    *   What did you glean from your *lectio divina*? (Day 4)

3. If there is time, continue the discussion around any of these questions:

    *   List some of the ways you began to develop the habit of prayer. Did you create a special place for prayer or set aside definite times? If so, describe.

    *   What are some of the benefits of spending time in prayer? How does this compare with times when you neglect to pray?

Session Five Outline

DVD Presentation: "Walking in Prayerfulness"

This video session will prepare you to take the first step in walking more consciously in prayer. Add your notes to the talk outline below.

I. Introduction

    a. CCC 2560 – Prayer is the encounter of God's thirst with ours

    b. Christian prayer is unique because it reflects a filial relationship

II. Definition of Prayer

    a. CCC 2559

    b. Prayer as a drama of the heart

    c. Prayer as a willed habit

        i. St. Teresa of Avila: "Anyone who does not pray does not need the devil to tempt them."

    d. CCC 2567 – Prayer is our response to God's call

    e. Prayer is fully revealed in Jesus Christ

III. The Drama of Prayer Revealed in Christ

    a. Jesus learned to pray

    b. Jesus' prayer was filial: Matthew 6:9

    c. Jesus prayed before decisive moments

    d. Jesus took time to be alone with his Father

        i. Luke 5:16; 11:1

        ii. CCC 2602

        iii. Content of prayer revealed in words and works

IV. Three Principle Parables on Prayer

   a. Luke 11:5-13 – The Persistent Friend

   b. Luke 18:1-8 – The Persistent Widow

   c. Luke 18:9-14 – The Pharisee and the Tax Collector

V. The Lord's Prayer

   a. Two fundamental dispositions (CCC 2800)

      i. Desire to be like Jesus

      ii. Have a humble, trusting, childlike heart

   b. We are not just individuals; we are a family

   c. Seven petitions

      i. CCC 2804 – First three focus on God

      ii. CCC 2805 – Last four focus on our needs

VI. Types of Prayer

   a. Example of making prayer a priority: Joe

   b. Blessings (CCC 2626) and adoration (CCC 2628)

   c. Prayer of Petition

   d. Prayer of Intercession

VII. Expressions of Prayer

   a. Vocal prayer

   b. Mental prayer

      i. St. Augustine: "A certain quietude is a requirement of the mind."

   c. Contemplative Prayer

    i.   St. Teresa of Avila: Contemplation is "a close sharing between friends" (*The Book of Her Life*, 8, 5)

    ii.   St. John Vianney: "I look at our Lord in the tabernacle, and he looks at me."

VIII. Suggestions

a.   Start by praying a little bit each day

b.   Choose a time and place to pray

c.   Learn to pray the Scriptures *(lectio divina)*

    i.   Psalms

    ii.   The Lord's Prayer (Matthew 6)

    iii.   St. Teresa of Avila: Take a book with you to prayer

d.   Learn to pray the Rosary

e.   Sign up for a Holy Hour

f.   Keep a prayer journal

    i.   Write down your thoughts

    ii.   Write down others' intentions

    iii.   Write down your own intentions, requests, prayers

        a.) How you want to change

        b.) Your needs

Quiet Time in the Lord's Presence

This is an opportunity for you to sit and pray silently in Christ's presence, allowing him to speak to your heart about how you can grow in prayer. Respond by committing to a specific step you will take to bring about a needed change in your life. **Follow the guidelines on the next page.**

Remember, mental acknowledgement that change is needed is not change. Action – responding in word and deed – is essential for lasting change.

"Be renewed in the spirit of your minds, and put on the new man, created after the likeness of God in true righteousness and holiness."

– Ephesians 4:23-24

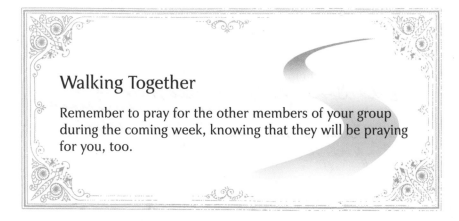

Walking Together

Remember to pray for the other members of your group during the coming week, knowing that they will be praying for you, too.

My Step for This Week:

1. I believe the Lord is asking me to walk more prayerfully in this area of my life:

   Using my prayer time & going to my private prayer area to pray.

2. Specifically, I am going to do the following this week:

   Spend time in front of the Blessed Sacrament, in meditative prayer.

3. I will take the necessary first step on

   _____.

   (day and time)

4. My prayer for help:

   Oh God help me to meditate on Your Sacred Body in the Tabernacle. Guide me in my meditative prayer

six

WALKING IN FAITHFULNESS

"*God doesn't ask that we succeed in everything, but that we are faithful. However beautiful our work may be, let us not become attached to it. Always remain prepared to give it up, without losing your peace.*"

– Blessed Teresa of Calcutta (Mother Teresa)

DAY 1

Date *Thurs 6/7*

The Meaning of Faithfulness

Pray before you begin. Ask the Lord to show you what faithfulness truly means.

1. How does the dictionary define "faithfulness"?

   True to ones word, promise, vows reliable, trusted or believed worthy of trust or belief

2. The Bible reveals God to be the greatest example of faithfulness. To understand what this means, read the following verses aloud. Read each one again slowly. Repeat it in your mind and think about what it says. After each verse, write down the words, phrases, or concepts about faithfulness that most stand out to you.

   a. Deuteronomy 7:9 *faithful. God those who love him keep his commandments merciful covenant down to thouserath generatn*

   b. Romans 3:3-4 *God must be true*

   c. 2 Thessalonians 3:3

   Lord is faithful he will strengthen you + guard you

   d. Micah 7:18-20

   God removes guilt - pardons sins compassion on us show faithfulness

3. Circle the word or phrase you wrote down in Question 2 that speaks most to you. Why did you choose it?

   Deuteronomy 7:9 God will be merciful + faithful you all who love him and keep his commandments

4. How has God's faithfulness sustained you over the years? List some concrete examples.

at time of parents death

divorce

James accident (s)

> "How does God demonstrate his faithfulness?"

He keeps forgiving us no matter how many times we need to be forgiven.

We are always getting blessings from God.

> "God, who reveals his name as
> 'I AM,' reveals himself as the God
> who is always there, present to his
> people in order to save them."
>
> – *Catechism* 207

Optional Further Reading

a. Lamentations 3:22-23 *favors renewed each morning favors of Lord not exhausted*

b. Psalm 33:4
Lord's word is true Lord's word is trustworthy

c. 1 Corinthians 1:9
called to fellowship w/ Jesus God is faithful

d. Psalm 119:89-90
Your word Lord stands forever truth endures

e. Hebrews 11:1
Faith is realization of what is hoped for Faith is evidence of what is not seen

DAY 2

Date *Sat 6/10*

The Importance of Being Faithful

Pray before you begin. Ask the Lord to show you the importance of being faithful.

1. What happens to relationships when faithfulness is not present (marriage, friendship, work situations)?

   Relationships struggle, tensions arise, one becomes suspicious of other person in relationship - lack of communication grows - Relationships then fail

2. Discover what the Bible has to say about the importance of walking in faithfulness. First, read the following verses aloud. Then read each one again slowly. Repeat it in your mind and think about what it says. After each verse, write down the words, phrases, or concepts that most stand out to you.

   a. Proverbs 3:3 *fidelity + kindness - not leave you. keep near close*

   b. Matthew 25:21 *good + faithful servant share masters joy faithful in small matters, leads to great responsibilities*

   c. 1 Samuel 26:23 *reward for justice + faithfulness not harm Lords anointed*

   d. Revelation 2:10 *faithful until death do not be afraid*

3. Why do people have such a difficult time remaining faithful in today's society?

In todays society a lot of people act that if something such as a marriage has difficulties one should just give up. Instead of looking at the root of the problem & trying to solve the problem.

We must believe. Do what the Church teaches.

"God loves us with a definitive and irrevocable love, … married couples share in this love, … it supports and sustains them, and … by their own faithfulness they can be witnesses to God's faithful love."

– *Catechism* 1648

Optional Further Reading

a. Hosea 2:20 *make a covenant rest in security*

b. Isaiah 46:11

c. Luke 16:10-12 *trustworthy in small matters – trustworthy in great one dishonest in small matters – dishonest in great matters*

DAY 3

Date *Sun 6/10*

Walking in Faithfulness

Pray before you begin. Ask the Lord to show you what it means to follow him by walking in faithfulness.

1. According to the Bible, what does it mean to walk in faithfulness? Prayerfully read the following verses several times and meditate on them. Record what stands out to you about being faithful.

    a. Romans 1:5 *receive grace of apostleship obedience of faith for the sake of his name*

    b. Proverbs 3:3 *don't lose kindness + fidelity keep him close*

    c. Proverbs 14:5 *truthful witness does not lie*

    d. 1 Timothy 3:11 *women - dignified - temperate and faithful*

2. Read the story of Ruth and Naomi in Ruth 1:1-18. What qualities of faithfulness do you see in Ruth? *will not abandon or forsake will go wherever you will go "your God will be my God"*

"Our life is full of brokenness – broken relationships, broken promises, broken expectations. How can we live with that brokenness without becoming bitter and resentful except by returning again and again to God's faithful presence in our lives?"

– Henri Nouwen

"What are some practical ways to walk in faithfulness?"

3. As you reflect on this story and the verses in Question 1, can you think of a way in which God is calling you to demonstrate faithfulness to him or to another person?

To be faithful to God by keeping close to Him through prayer and actions.

- *being witness to our faith + God*
- *being temperate*
- *keep God close through prayer + meditation*

4. What obstacles or feelings of resistance come up for you when you think about how you are being called to walk in faithfulness?

Obstacles would be when questioned about the Church + what we believe + unable or unwilling to get into an "arguement" because of lack of knowledge or rather lack of ability to defend with specific details why something is or why we do something

Optional Further Reading

a. Daniel 6:4 *no grounds for accusations except for the law of God*

b. Psalm 85:10 *salvation for the loyal prosperity fill our land (our soul)*

c. 2 Timothy 2:11-13 *died w/ him → live with Him persevere → will reign with him he remains faithful because He cannot deny Himself*

DAY 4   *Date* _____

Praying Scripture For A Change

Pray before you begin. Ask the Lord to show you in what areas he can help you to be faithful.

1. Look back through your journal for the week and select the Scripture that meant the most to you. Look it up in your Bible and decide whether to read it alone or in the context of the surrounding passage.

Write the verse and its reference here:

> Psalm 85:10
> 9 I will listen for the word of God
> surely the LORD will proclaim peace
> to his people, to the faithful, to
> those who trust in him.
> 10 Near indeed is salvation for the
> loyal; prosperity will fill our
> land.

2. Using the steps of *lectio divina*, meditate on the Scripture you chose until it turns into prayer and then simply rest in the Lord, trusting that he will help you to take action and make a change in your life.

Read *(Lectio)*

Meditate *(Meditatio)*

"What did you glean from your *lectio divina?*"

Pray *(Oratio)*

Contemplate *(Contemplatio)*

Resolve to Act *(Operatio)*

MEETING DAY

Date _____

Taking the First Step

Small Group Discussion

This is the time to share the insights you received this past week and hear from the other members in the group. You will begin with a group exercise of lectio divina.

1. Meditate prayerfully as a group on **Luke 16:10-12.** (Choose three people to look up the passage and read it out loud as described on page 12.)

2. Answer these questions as a group, sharing insights gleaned from the verses you meditated on this week. (Turn back in your journal to recall what you discovered each day, and use the space provided to add new insights from the group discussion.)

   • How does God demonstrate his faithfulness? (Day 1)

   • Why is faithfulness important in relationships? (Day 2)

   • What are some practical ways to walk in faithfulness? (Day 3)

   • What did you glean from your *lectio divina* on Day 4?

3. If there is time, continue the discussion around any of these questions:

   • Is there someone in your life who has consistently demonstrated faithfulness? Describe how.

   • How might you demonstrate faithfulness in the workplace?

Session Six Outline

DVD Presentation: "Walking in Faithfulness"

This video session will prepare you to take the first step in walking more consciously in faithfulness. Add your notes to the talk outline below.

I. Introduction

   a. Size, prominence of act less important than faithfulness

   b. Not, "Are you willing to die for your loved ones?" but "Will you live for your family faithfully?" *on a daily basis are you willing to live faithfully for your family*

II. Faithfulness Defined

   a. Heb. *emunah*: "steadiness, fidelity, faithfulness" *as long as* (Example: Exodus 17:12) *Moses held his hands up Israel was winning the battle when his arms got tired Aaron + Hur held them up – steadiness.*

   b. God is <u>faithful</u> and <u>worthy of trust</u>

      i. 1 Corinthians 1:9 *God is faithful called to fellowship with his Son*

      ii. 2 Timothy 2:13 *if we are faithless, God is still faithful*

      iii. Deuteronomy 7:9 *he is a Father he is a faithful Father merciful down to thousand all generations*

      iv. Psalm 145:13 *faithful in all his words*

III. Jesus: The Faithful Son

   a. Jesus entrusted himself to his Father's faithfulness *Jesus not only entrusted himself to Mary + Joseph, but also to his Father*

      i. Psalm 31:5 *God is our refuge*

      ii. Hebrews 3:5-6 *we are all in God's house as a Son/Daughter*

iii. Matthew 6:6 *pray in secret & your Father see you in private*

b. The basis of our faithfulness: God's faithfulness *hope based on something beyond concrete – based on God's faithfulness*

   i. Habakkuk 2:4 *will live by his faithfulness*

   ii. CCC 346 *In Creation God established laws that remain firm (ie gravity)*

   iii. 1 Samuel 17:37 *David " God will keep me safe."*

   iv. CCC 2592 *battle of faith marked by trust in God's faithfulness*

c. Example of faithfulness: The Daly family

IV. The Creed *reaffirms our faithfulness & belief*

a. "Believe" as a key to understanding the Creed (CCC 150) *• personal adherence of man to God • entrust oneself wholly to God*

b. Two aspects to "I believe"

   i. Intellectual

   ii. Entrusting oneself to God *Act of will*

c. Heb. *Amen* from same root as "believe" *I am entrusting myself to you.*

   i. CCC 1062, 1064 *"Amen" expresses God's faithfulness towards us & our trust in him*

   ii. "To take my stand on someone else" (Pope Benedict XVI) *I am taking my stand on someone else. – esp. Jesus.*

V. Key Aspects of Faithfulness

a. Attentiveness to small things – Matthew 25:21 *hope*

"Amen" "I believe" "to God's word, promises & commandments" entrust myself completely to Him

b. A life of obedience to God – John 6:38
    doing what God wants us to do

c. Making decisions based on God's Word – Psalm 119:30
    Sacred Scripture
    Sacred Teaching

d. Honesty – Proverbs 27:6
    faithful are wounds of a friend
    pray for enemy

e. Loyalty (Example: David's faithfulness to Saul)

f. Dependability – Psalm 15:4; Proverbs 11:13
    keeps their promises even if it is difficult

g. Not compromising
    faithful
    familial spousal relationship w/ God

h. Example of spousal faithfulness as a witness to God's love: Betty

    i. CCC 1648
        loyalty + faithfulness

VI. Conclusion

a. Archbishop Fulton Sheen – "Little things make up the universe…"

b. God chooses the weak to show forth his faithfulness (CCC 489)

"Be faithful in God's time + in bad times"

Quiet Time in the Lord's Presence

This is an opportunity for you to sit and pray silently in Christ's presence, allowing him to speak to your heart about how you can grow in faithfulness. Respond by committing to a specific step you will take to bring about a needed change in your life. **Follow the guidelines on the next page.**

Remember, mental acknowledgement that change is needed is not change. Action – responding in word and deed – is essential for lasting change.

> *"Be renewed in the spirit of your minds, and put on the new man, created after the likeness of God in true righteousness and holiness."*
>
> *– Ephesians 4:23-24*

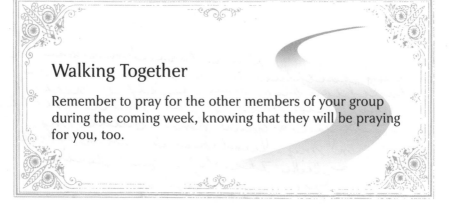

Walking Together

Remember to pray for the other members of your group during the coming week, knowing that they will be praying for you, too.

My Step for This Week:

1. I believe the Lord is asking me to walk more faithfully in this area of my life:

   To spend more time in meditation & following His guidance

2. Specifically, I am going to do the following this week:

3. I will take the necessary first step on

   _____.

   (day and time)

4. My prayer for help: *Dear Lord Thank you for being faithful to me even when I have doubted my faithfulness to you. Help me to be more faithful to you & your Son. Guide me in my relationship with others & live the life you desire for me. Amen.*

seven

WALKING IN SACRIFICE

"Jesus says: 'My daughter… You will save more souls through prayer and suffering than will a missionary through his teachings and sermons alone. I want to see you as a sacrifice of living love, which only then carries weight before me… Outwardly, your sacrifice must look like this: silent, hidden, permeated with love, imbued with prayer… I will not spare my grace, that you may be able to fulfill what I demand of you.'"

– St. Maria Faustina Kowalska

DAY 1

Date *June 14*

The Meaning of Sacrifice

Pray before you begin. Ask the Lord to show you what sacrifice truly means.

1. Look up the word "sacrifice" in the dictionary. How is sacrifice defined?

    · giving up of something precious
    · an act of offering to a diety
       something precious

2. Discover what the Bible has to say about sacrifice. Read the
    following verses aloud. Read each one again slowly. Repeat it in
    your mind and think about what it says. After each verse, write
    down the words, phrases, or concepts that most stands out to you.

    a. Psalm 51:19 *proclaim your praise*

    b. Romans 12:1 *spiritual worship*
        offer bodies as a living sacrifice

    ✻c. Ephesians 5:2
        live in love as Christ loved us

    d. Luke 22:42
        not my will but yours be done

3. Circle the word or phrase you wrote down in Question 2 that
    speaks most to you. Why did you choose it?

    Ephesians 5:2
    ...and live in love as Christ loved us
    and handed himself over for us as
    a sacrificial offering to God for a
    fragrant of aroma

    That I should try to love everyone
    as Christ loved us; and that we
    should offer spiritual sacrifices

4. Think of a favorite saint or martyr. How did that person demonstrate the meaning of sacrifice portrayed in one of these verses?

St. Bernadette – she lived her life with a love of the Blessed Virgin + offering up her suffering in silence

"Outward sacrifice, to be genuine, must be the expression of spiritual sacrifice… The only perfect sacrifice is the one that Christ offered on the cross as a total offering to the Father's love and for our salvation. By uniting ourselves with his sacrifice we can make our lives a sacrifice to God."

– *Catechism* 2100

Optional Further Reading:

a. 2 Corinthians 5:15 *he indeed died for all. those who live might no longer live for themselves but for Him*

b. Psalm 141:2 *Let my prayers be incense on evening sacrifice*

c. Proverbs 21:3 *• do what is right + just • more acceptable … than sacrifice*

DAY 2   Date _June 16_

The Importance of Sacrifice

Pray before you begin. Ask the Lord to show you the importance of sacrifice.

1. Describe a marriage that is devoid of sacrifice. What results when a couple chooses selfishness over sacrifice? *When one of the people involved in a marriage chose his/her desires over the good for the couple or family. The faithfulness that the couple promised each other at their marriage is not there anymore - + the marriage starts to "fall apart." One of the people involved usually has to sacrifice many things maybe even their own self-confidence or self-worth to try one keep the marriage together*

2. Keeping in mind the meaning of sacrifice you discovered on Day 1, what are some sacrifices you have had to make in your own life? What has your attitude been toward them? *I had to sacrifice my self esteem at the time of my divorce. I wondered what I had done wrong, what more I could have done to keep the marriage together. It hurt even more when he said he still loved me, but didn't want to be married anymore. Before that I think I sacrificed James' well-being by not seeking help at Al-anon, because Bob said he would leave me I did anything like that. He left anyway.*

> "It is right to offer sacrifice to God as a sign of adoration and gratitude, supplication and communion: 'Every action done so as to cling to God in communion of holiness, and thus achieve blessedness, is a true sacrifice.'"
>
> – *Catechism* 2099

I felt hurt + betrayed because I still loved him + would have done anything to keep the marriage together. I didn't like maybe even hated, at times, +

+ what he did + how he did it. My attitude is that I have forgiven him + I still love the person I fell in love with originally

· setting on example
· growing in commitment

3. Discover what the Bible has to say about the importance of sacrifice. First, read the following verses aloud. Then read each one again slowly. Repeat it in your mind and think about what it says. After each verse, write down the words, phrases, or concepts that most stand out to you.

    a. Matthew 19:27-30 *everyone who has given up ... will inherit eternal life*

    b. Hebrews 5:8
        learned obedience suffered.

    c. John 12:24-26
        · honor who ever serves
        · me
        · ?

Optional Further Reading

    a. Colossians 1:24 *in my flesh filling up what is lacking · rejoice in my suffering*

    b. Ruth 2:11-12
        Lord rewards what you have done

    c. Luke 9:23 *follow me take up his cross daily*

    d. Hebrews 10:34
        joined in his suffering better + lasting possessions

DAY 3   *Date* _____

Walking in Sacrifice

Pray before you begin. Ask the Lord to show you what it means to follow him by walking in sacrifice.

1. According to the Bible, what does it mean to walk in sacrifice? Prayerfully read the following verses several times and meditate on them. Record what stands out to you about sacrifice.

    a. Hebrews 13:15-16 *offer God a sacrifice of praise*
        * *do not neglect to do good*
        * *share what we have*
        * *God is pleased with sacrifices*
    b. Mark 8:34
        * *follow me*
        * *come after me must deny himself*

    c. 2 Corinthians 4:8-10 *life of Christ may also be manifested in our body*
        * *we are afflicted*

2. Read the story of Abraham and Isaac in Genesis 22:1-14. How did Abraham respond when God asked him to sacrifice his son? How did God respond to Abraham's obedience?

    God asked Abraham to sacrifice his son Isaac. He was willing to obey God without question. Since he was willing to sacrifice his son God allowed Isaac to live because Abraham had shown his faith in God

3. As you reflect on this story and the verses in Question 1, why do you think God would require sacrifice from us? What is your response when circumstances don't turn out the way you envisioned them?

    God tests us so we can prove our faith + love in Him.

"What are some practical ways to walk in sacrifice?"

Weak as I am, I question why am I being forced to go through this sacrifice. Through prayer I have kept my faith that God has some ulterior motive behind my sacrifice

- serve others
- charity work
- Corporal Works of Mercy

4. What obstacles or feelings of resistance come up for you when you think about things you are being called to offer up or places you are being called walk in sacrifice?

It all comes back to my selfishness for my time. Fear of what God is calling me to do + working to overcome this need feeling in my life to spend more time in prayer to disters my thoughts.

Optional Further Reading

a. Jonah 2:9 *source of mercy*

b. 1 Peter 2:4-5 *spiritual sacrifice*
   - let yourself be built into a spiritual house
   - chosen + precious in the sight of God

*c. Ephesians 3:13
   not to lose heart
   this is your glory

d. 2 Timothy 1:8
   - do not be ashamed of your testimony to our Lord
   - strength that comes from God

DAY 4   *Date* _____

Praying Scripture for a Change

Pray before you begin. Ask the Lord to show you in what areas he can help you to offer something up in a sacrificial way.

1. Look back through your journal for the week and select the Scripture verse that meant the most to you. Look it up in your Bible and decide whether to read it alone or in the context of the surrounding passage.

Write the verse and its reference here:

> Psalm 141:2
> Let my prayer be incense before you; my uplifted hands an evening sacrifice.

2. Using the steps of *lectio divina*, meditate on the Scripture you chose until it turns into prayer and then simply rest in the Lord, trusting that he will help you to take action and make a change in your life.

Read *(Lectio)*

Meditate *(Meditatio)*

"What did you glean from your *lectio divina*?"

Pray *(Oratio)*

Contemplate *(Contemplatio)*

Resolve to Act *(Operatio)*

MEETING DAY

Taking the First Step

Small Group Discussion

This is the time to share the insights you received this past week and hear from the other members in the group. You will begin with a group exercise of lectio divina.

1. Meditate prayerfully as a group on **John 12:24-26.** (Choose three people to look up the passage and read it out loud as described on page 12.)

2. Answer these questions as a group, sharing insights gleaned from the verses you meditated on this week. (Turn back in your journal to recall what you discovered each day, and use the space provided to add new insights from the group discussion.):

    •   What is sacrifice? (Day 1)

    •   Why is sacrifice important? (Day 2)

    •   What are some practical ways to walk in sacrifice? (Day 3)

    •   What did you glean from your *lectio divina*? (Day 4)

3. If there is time, continue the discussion around any of these questions:

    •   How did your definition of sacrifice and its importance change or expand?

    •   Did you observe any real-life examples of someone walking in sacrifice?

    •   What insights did you gain about areas in your life where sacrifice is asked of you?

Session Seven Outline

DVD Presentation: "Walking in Sacrifice"

This video session will prepare you to take the first step in walking more consciously in sacrifice. Add your notes to the talk outline below.

I. Introduction

    a. We are to be "living sacrifices" out of love for Christ (Romans 12:1)

    b. Suffering can be part of sacrifice

II. A Definition of Sacrifice

    a. Elements brought to God to express devotion, thanksgiving, repentance

    b. Old Testament sacrifices

III. Christ: The Ultimate and Definitive Sacrifice

    a. Jesus' death is described in sacrificial terms

        i. The sinless high priest (Hebrews 4:14-5:10)

        ii. The paschal lamb (1 Corinthians 5:7)

Christ our paschal lamb has been sacrificed

    b. Need for sacrifices ceases, except for thank offerings *(todah)*

        i. Jesus prophesies destruction of Temple (Matthew 24:1-8)

        ii. The Holy Sacrifice of the Mass; the Eucharist

IV. Christ's Death Is the Appeal for a Christian's Sacrifice

    a. Our sacrifices are an expression of his

        i. Filling up Christ's sacrifice (Colossians 1:24)

rejoice in my suffering

    ii. Jesus makes room for us to participate in his loving sacrifice for the world (Blessed John Paul II)

    iii. Offer ourselves as a living sacrifice (Romans 12:1)

    iv. We are "crucified with Christ" (Galatians 2:20)

    v. Radical identification with Christ (2 Corinthians 5:15)

    no longer live for themselves

  b. Choice: live for selves or live for Christ

    i. "I die daily" (1 Corinthians 15:31)

    be witnesses to faith

    doing good for others daily

  c. Acts 1:8 – "You shall be witnesses" (*martys*)

  d. Example of loving sacrifice: Jon

V. Ideal Life Meets Real Life

Ideal - comfortable, predictable, painfree, accomplished at

  a. The difference between "ideal" and "real"

Real - uncomfortable, unpredictable

  b. When real meets ideal:

    i. Others pay the price

    ii. No peace or joy

    iii. Don't provide our children with a good example

    iv. We retreat from reality

    v. We blame others

    vi. We self-medicate

    vii. We objectify others

    viii. We live a partial life

  c. Live in joy and peace: offer your life to God as living sacrifice

VI. Accepting Divine Providence

    a. "If the Lord wills" (James 4:14-15)
        you shall live to do this or that

    b. John 21:18 *when young do for yourself*
        . when older you are lead where you dont

    c. All of life has value *want to go*

VII. Finding Meaning in Suffering

    a. Blessed John Paul II on suffering *(Salvifici Doloris)*

        i. Two kinds, physical and <u>moral</u>– *suffering in the heart*

        ii. Two types, temporal and <u>definitive</u> *suffering eternally*
        w/out our Lord

    b. Christ used suffering to deal with suffering

    c. Offer it up – your "real life" has redemptive power
        if you are suffering offer it up fo
        others

    d. Christ's life manifest in mortal flesh (2 Corinthians 4:8-11, 14)
        the life of Jesus may also be manifested
        in our body

VIII. Suggestions for Walking in Sacrifice

    a. Don't live for self only *love opens up your world*
        . The will that lives for ones self loses
        ones self.

    b. Live a life of service

    c. See weakness as an opportunity to be perfected
        (2 Corinthians 12:9) *power of Christ may dwell*
        with me.

        My grace is sufficient for you
    d. Make each sacrifice into an expression of your love

IX. Conclusion

Quiet Time in the Lord's Presence

This is an opportunity for you to sit and pray silently in Christ's presence, allowing him to speak to your heart about how you can walk in sacrifice in new ways. Respond by committing to a specific step you will take to bring about a needed change in your life.

Remember, mental acknowledgement that change is needed is not change. Action – responding in word and deed – is essential for lasting change.

"Be renewed in the spirit of your minds, and put on the new man, created after the likeness of God in true righteousness and holiness"

– Ephesians 4:23-24

Walking Together

Remember to pray for the other members of your group during the coming week, knowing that they will be praying for you, too.

My Step for This Week:

1. I believe the Lord is asking me to walk in sacrifice toward this person (or in this situation) my life:

2. Specifically, I am going to do the following this week:

3. I will take the necessary first step on

    _____.
    (day and time)

4. My prayer for help:

eight

WALKING IN THANKFULNESS

*"If the only prayer you said in your whole life was 'thank you,'
that would suffice."*

— *Meister Eckhart*

DAY 1

Date *Thursday 6/31*

The Meaning of Thankfulness

Pray before you begin. Ask the Lord to show you what thankfulness truly means.

1. What does thankfulness mean to you, and how do you tend to express it?

   Being grateful for something done for you or given you
   Returning love through a "gift" not necessarily monetary. A simple "thank you" says more than doing anything – just being there physically or in thought

2. Discover what the Bible has to say about thankfulness: Read the following verses aloud. Read each one again slowly. Repeat it in your mind and think about what it says. After each verse, write down the words, phrases, or concepts that most stand out to you.

   a. Psalm 50:23 *sacrifice honor me obedient ... show salvation of God*

   b. Hebrews 13:15
   don't neglect to do good God is pleased

   c. 1 Timothy 4:4
   received w/ thanksgiving everything created by God is good

   ✱ d. Psalm 107:8
   thank the Lord for such kindness wonderous deeds for mere mortals

3. Circle the word or phrase you wrote down in Question 2 that speaks most to you. Why did you choose it?

   Psalm 107:8. Let them thank the Lord for such kindness, such wonderous deeds for mere mortals

   That I (we) need to constantly thank the Lord for everything he has given and done for us. Unworthy as we may be.

4. Why does God deserve our thankfulness? List some reasons to respond to God with thanksgiving.

God deserves our thankfulness for all that He has done + given us.

• He is all forgiving

• He sent his Son to us as an example to live like

• He sacrificed his Son

• The opportunity to receive him in the Eucharist

"Praise is the form of prayer which recognizes most immediately that God is God. It lauds God for his own sake and gives him glory, quite beyond what he does, but simply because HE IS."

– Catechism 2639

"Eucharist means first of all 'thanksgiving.'"

– Catechism 1360

Optional Further Reading

a. Hebrews 12:28 *reverence + awe*
   • gratitude
   • we who are receiving the unshakeable kingdom

b. Psalm 75:1
   • we thank you God; we give thanks
   • we call upon your name
   • declare your wonderful deeds

c. Psalm 92:1
   • Thanks to the Lord
   • praise your name • I shout for joy
   • proclaim your love
   • you make me jubilant

Psalm 75:10 I will rejoice forever I will sing praises to the God of Jacob

DAY 2

Date Saturday
6/23

The Importance of Being Thankful

Pray before you begin. Ask the Lord to show you the importance of being thankful.

1. What are some of the consequences of not being thankful?

    People do not think you appreciate what they have done for you. Hard feelings can develop - that possibly ruin a friendship

2. Keeping in mind the meaning of thankfulness you discovered on Day 1, how might being thankful change the way you look at tough situations in your life?

    Being thankful can get you through tough times - thanking those who were/are there for you. Thanking God because he had a reason - unknown to you at the time - but knowing he has a plan for you.

"Believing in God, the only One, and loving him with all our being has enormous consequences for our whole life... *It means living in thanksgiving:* if God is the only One, everything we are and have comes from him: 'What have you that you did not receive?' 'What shall I render to the Lord for all his bounty to me?'"

– *Catechism 222-224*

3. Discover what the Bible has to say about the importance of thankfulness. First, read the following verses aloud. Then read each one again slowly. Repeat it in your mind and think about what it says. After each verse, write down the words, phrases, or concepts that most stand out to you.

  a. 1 Thessalonians 5:16-18

    pray without ceasing
    all circumstances give thanks
    will of God

  b. Colossians 2:6-7

    received Christ Jesus
    established in the faith
    abound in thanksgiving

  c. Philippians 4:8

    • anything worthy of praise
    think of these things

Optional Further Reading

  a. Revelation 19:4-5 *worshipped God*
    praise our God
    you who revere Him

  b. Psalm 118:24.

    rejoice
    be glad

  c. James 1:17

    all good giving ...
    from above

  d. 2 Corinthians 9:15

    thanks be to God.
    indescribable gifts

DAY 3

Date *Sunday 6/24*

Walking in Thankfulness

Pray before you begin. Ask the Lord to show you what it means to follow him by walking in thankfulness.

1. According to the Bible, what does it mean to walk in thankfulness? Prayerfully read these verses several times each and meditate on them. Record what stands out to you about thankfulness.

    a. Ephesians 5:15,19-20 *watch how you live... be wise*
        - *give thanks always for everything*
        - *sing & play to the Lord in your hearts*
        - *address one another in psalms, hymns & song*
    b. Colossians 3:15-17
        - *sing psalms, hymns & spiritual songs w/ gratitude*
        - *peace be Christ control your heart* •*Be thankful*
        - *let the word of Christ dwell in you richly*
    c. 1 Chronicles 16:8
        - *give thanks*
        - ~~invoke~~ *invoke his name*

2. Read the story of Jesus healing the ten lepers in Luke 17:11-19. What was Jesus' response when he encountered the ten lepers who asked him for mercy? How does this relate to your need for Jesus' intervention in difficulties you face? When the time of crisis has passed, what is your response?

    "Go show yourselves to the priests" ~
    "Ten were cleaned were they not? Where are the other 9? Has none but this foreigner returned to give thanks to God?"

    When in a difficult situation the common response is to ask for God's help such as "please help me get through this situation". When the crisis has passed thanks through prayer or sacrifice should be offered to God.

"What are some practical ways to walk in thankfulness, especially when you don't feel like it?"

3. What obstacles or feelings of resistance come up for you when you think about being thankful in *all* things?

   An obstacle would be that the situation may not be solved as we want, but as God wants to be. So being thankful will be thankful.

   "Not my will, but thy will be done"

4. What are some practical ways you might cultivate the habit of thankfulness?

   • get in the habit of praying regularly + in a specific space
   • ask for the intercession of Mary + the saints
   • go out of comfort zone

"For Christians, a special gratitude is due to those from whom they have received the gift of faith, the grace of baptism, and life in the Church."

– *Catechism* 2220

Optional Further Reading

a. Psalm 107:8
   thank the Lord for kindness

b. Psalm 34:1
   bless the Lord at all times praise ... always

c. James 5:13
   he should pray sing praise

d. Psalm 100:2-5 *worship the Lord w/ cries of gladness*
   • joyful song
   • enter with praise
   • give thanks to God

love endures forever

DAY 4

Praying Scripture for a Change

Pray before you begin. Ask the Lord to show you in what areas he can help you to walk in thankfulness.

1. Look back through your journal for the week and select the Scripture verse that meant the most to you. Look it up in your Bible and decide whether to read it alone or in the context of the surrounding passage.

Write the verse and its reference here:

Colossians 3:15-17
And let the peace of Christ control your
hearts... and be thankful. Let the
word of Christ dwell in you richly...
And whatever you do in word or in
deed, do everything in the name of
the Lord Jesus, giving thanks to
God the Father through him.

2. Using the steps of *lectio divina*, meditate on the Scripture you chose until it turns into prayer and then simply rest in the Lord, trusting that he will help you to take action and make a change in your life.

Read *(Lectio)*

Meditate *(Meditatio)*

Pray *(Oratio)*

Contemplate *(Contemplatio)*

Resolve to Act *(Operatio)*

MEETING DAY   *Date* _____

Taking The First Step

Small Group Discussion

This is the time to share the insights you received this past week and hear from the other members in the group. You will begin with a group exercise of lectio divina.

1. Meditate prayerfully as a group on **Colossians 3:15-17.** (Choose three people to look up the passage and read it out loud as described on page 12.)

2. Answer these questions as a group, sharing insights gleaned from the verses you meditated on this week. (Turn back in your journal to recall what you discovered each day, and use the space provided to add new insights from the group discussion.):

    •   What does it mean to be thankful? (Day 1)

    •   Why is thankfulness important? (Day 2)

    •   What are some practical ways to walk in thankfulness, especially when you don't feel like it? (Day 3)

    •   What did you glean from your *lectio divina*? (Day 4)

3. If there is time, continue the discussion around any of these questions:

    •   Why is thankfulness an important part of prayer?

    •   Was there a time during the week that someone expressed thankfulness to you? How did that make you feel?

    •   If you were able to express thankfulness in a tangible way for a particular person or event in your life, what was the result?

Session Eight Outline

DVD Presentation: *"Walking in Thankfulness"*

This video session will prepare you to take the first step in walking more consciously in thankfulness. Add your notes to the talk outline below.

I. Introduction

    a. The difference between praise and thanksgiving

        i. We praise God for who he is

        ii. We thank God for what he has done

II. Praise and Thanksgiving

    a. God still does mighty things

        i. Not by our might, but by God's power (Zechariah 4:6)

    b. Pattern of praise in Scripture

    c. Judah goes up first in battle

        i. Judah *(Yehudah)* means "to praise"

            a.) *Yadah* "to throw, to cast, to declare" *confess*

    d. God revealed in his works (CCC 236)

        i. Theology

        ii. Economy

    e. God's blessing manifest in saving events (CCC 1081)

III. Why Don't We Praise or Thank God?

    a. We don't know him

      i.   We don't remember his deeds (Psalm 75:1)

      ii. Our faith doesn't rest on his actions (CCC 2738)

  b. We don't trust him

      i.   Nominalism: God is arbitrary power

      ii. God's will informed by wisdom, not arbitrary (CCC 271)

      iii. History teaches us to trust God (CCC 304)

IV. Praise and Thanks in the Midst of Battle

  a. Psalm 106:1-2

  b. David (1 Samuel 7:41-47)

  c. Jehoshaphat (2 Chronicles 20)

V. Praise and Thanksgiving Doesn't Change God; It Changes Us!

  a. Thanksgiving is gratitude's natural expression

  b. The Ten Lepers (Luke 17:11-19)

  c. The secret to happiness is gratitude (G.K. Chesterton)

  d. Ingratitude indicates a heart turned in on itself

  e. Example of thankfulness: Michael

VI. The Eucharist: the Great Example of Praise and Thanksgiving

  a. The Eucharistic prayer (CCC 1352)

  b. Thanks mentioned many times

VII. Ten Ways to Walk in Thankfulness

  a. Enthrone God on your praise – Psalm 22:3

b. Put on the garment of praise – Isaiah 61:3

c. Express praise and thanksgiving

d. Every hour, find something to thank God for

    i. In suffering and joy, give thanks

        a.) CCC 2648

        b.) 1 Thessalonians 5:18

e. Set aside time daily

    i. Levites' practice: 1 Chronicles 23:30

    ii. Daniel 6:10

    iii. Set your watch

f. Count your blessings

g. Cultivate a life of thanksgiving

    i. Helps against anxiety, worry

    ii. Give thanks when you can't sleep (Psalm 119:62)

h. Show gratitude and thankfulness to others – think of three people

    i. Thank those who taught you the faith (CCC 2220)

    ii. Take care of your parents (CCC 2215)

i. Thank God for small and ordinary things

j. Fully participate in the Mass (the Great Thank Offering)

Quiet Time in the Lord's Presence

This is an opportunity for you to sit and pray silently in Christ's presence, allowing him to speak to your heart about how you can walk in thankfulness in new ways. Respond by committing to a specific step you will take to bring about a needed change in your life.

Remember, mental acknowledgement that change is needed is not change. Action – responding in word and deed – is essential for lasting change.

> *"Be renewed in the spirit of your minds, and put on the new man, created after the likeness of God in true righteousness and holiness"*
>
> *– Ephesians 4:23-24*

Walking Together

Remember to pray for the other members of your group during the coming week, knowing that they will be praying for you, too.

My Step for This Week:

1.   I believe the Lord is asking me to walk in thankfulness toward this person (or in this situation) my life:

2.   Specifically, I am going to do the following this week:

3.   I will take the necessary first step on

_____.

(day and time)

4.   My prayer for help:

Bibliography

Dubay, Thomas, S.M. *Prayer Primer*. Cincinnati, OH: Servant, 2002.

Gray, Timothy. *Praying Scripture for a Change*. West Chester, PA: Ascension, 2009.

John Paul II, Blessed. *The Post-Synodal Apostolic Exhortations of John Paul II*. Huntington, IN: Our Sunday Visitor, 1998.

Kowalska, St. Faustina. *Diary of St. Maria Faustina Kowalski: Divine Mercy in My Soul*. Stockbridge, MA: Marian, 2003.

Lewis, C.S. *The Weight of Glory*. San Francisco, CA: HarperSanFransisco, 2001.

Nouwen, Henri. *Mornings with Henri J.M. Nouwen*. Ann Arbor, MI: Charis, 1997.

Teresa of Calcutta, Blessed (Mother Teresa). *One Heart Full of Love*. Ann Arbor, MI: Servant, 1984.

_____. *No Greater Love*. Novato, CA: New World Library, 1997.

_____. *The Joy in Living*. London: Hodder & Stoughton, 1997.

Thérèse of Lisieux, St. *The Story of a Soul*. Washington, D.C.: ICS, 1996.